BUSINESS PORTRAITS

FORD

Published by VGM Career Horizons,
a division of NTC Publishing Group,
4255 West Touhy Avenue
Lincolnwood (Chicago), Illinois 60646-1975, U.S.A.

Gould, William, 1947–
    VGM's business portraits: Ford/William Gould.
        p. cm. – (VGM's business portraits)
    Includes index.
    Summary: Introduces basic business concepts, using Ford Motor
Company as a case study.
    ISBN 0-8442-4777-4 (alk. paper)
    1. Ford Motor Company – Juvenile literature. 2. Automobile
industry and trade – United States – Juvenile literature. (1. Ford
Motor Company. 2. Automobile industry and trade.) I. Title.
II. Series.
HD9710.U54F634 1996
338.7′6292′0973–dc20   96-10233
                                                                CIP
                                                                 AC

Manufactured in the United Kingdom.

BUSINESS PORTRAITS
FORD

[VGM business portraits. Ford]

WILLIAM GOULD

VGM Career Horizons
a division of *NTC Publishing Group*
Lincolnwood, Illinois USA

ACKNOWLEDGMENT

Our thanks to Ford for providing us with copies of their annual reports and historical publications from which we drew information to develop a profile of the Company. Editorial comments made and conclusions reached by the author about general business practices of international companies do not necessarily reflect the policies and practices of the Ford Motor Company.

Our thanks to the following organizations for supplying additional photographs: Motor Industry Archive, National Motor Museum, Ogilvy and Mather, Peter Newark's American Pictures, Quadrant; and to the following individuals for supplying artwork: Malcolm Porter, Neil Reed, John York.

CONTENTS

The adventure of business.............................6

The Ford Motor Company 8

The man behind the motor 10

Third time lucky 12

Popular or luxury cars? 14

A car for the multitude 16

On the line 18

Competition 20

Working at Ford 22

How Ford manages 24

Selling Ford cars 26

Ford goes places 28

Fighting on new fronts 30

Branching out 32

Customer is king 34

Advertising 36

Technology and design 38

Ford in the community 40

The road ahead 42

Create your own business 44

The language of business 46

Index 48

Legend:
- People
- Money
- Things

▲ Businesses need people (human resources), things (physical resources) and money (capital).

▶ Ford produces vehicles for sale all round the world. To fight competition new models must be produced all the time and incorporate the latest technology – like the fiber-optic fog lights on this truck.

The adventure of business

Business often sounds difficult but its basic principles are simple, and it can be very exciting. The people involved in the creation and running of the businesses we examine in VGM'S BUSINESS PORTRAITS faced challenges and took risks that make some adventure stories seem dull.

The business of business

Anyone who produces goods or services in return for money is involved in business. Businesses come in all shapes and sizes. From hamburgers to holidays, businesses supply nearly all the goods and services we use every day.

Businesses try to make profits. They try to sell things for more than the amount the things cost to make. They usually invest part of the profit they make in producing or selling more of their product.

The business of Ford

Over the years Ford has become known for making vans, trucks, farm machinery, industrial engines, aerospace products and electronic goods. But the success of the Ford company has been built on its cars for ordinary people.

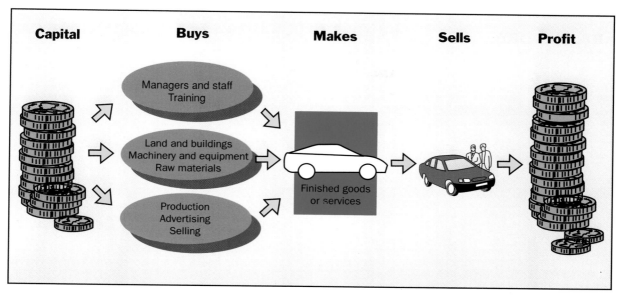

Capital	Buys	Makes	Sells	Profit

- Managers and staff / Training
- Land and buildings / Machinery and equipment / Raw materials
- Production / Advertising / Selling
- Finished goods or services

The language of business

Many of the technical terms that make the language of business sound complicated are explained on pages 46 and 47.

Business matters

Yellow panels throughout the book explain general business concepts. Blue panels tell you more about Ford.

▲ A business uses money to buy human and physical resources, and create a product or service that it sells for a profit.

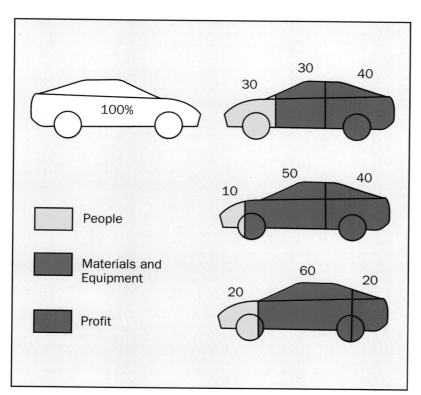

100%

30   30   40

10   50   40

20   60   20

People

Materials and Equipment

Profit

◄ The purpose of a business is to make a profit. Profit is the amount of money earned from sales after all the costs are paid. If a car costs $8,000 and sells for $10,000, the profit is $2,000.

Henry Ford was one of eight children born to Irish immigrants William and Mary Ford. Henry grew up to have a forceful personality with strong views. He led the Ford Motor Company for 42 years and revolutionized the making and selling of cars. But he was a controversial figure. In 1915 he sailed to Europe in a bid to stop World War I. The trip was ridiculed. But in 1917, when the United States entered the war, he turned his factories over to military production. In 1918 he ran for the US Senate but lost. In the same year he bought a newspaper, *The Dearborn Independent*, in which he made public his own anti-Jewish and other ideas. In 1927 he publicly took back what he had written. Henry Ford was capable of meanness and generosity – he funded a hospital for Detroit – and great errors of judgement. He was a complex character but when it came to cars he was a genius.

The Ford Motor Company

Almost everywhere you go you will find cars and trucks bearing the name "Ford." From its headquarters near Detroit, Michigan, USA, the Ford Motor Company has been manufacturing cars since 1903. It operates in 26 countries around the world and sells in more than 100. It has factories for building cars from scratch, and assembly plants where workers put together cars from parts made elsewhere. From these manufacturing centers, Ford turns out millions of cars every year.

A second, less well-known but important part of Ford's business is in financial services. The company gives credit to people buying or leasing its cars and other products. In addition, it is involved in other businesses, most of which are related to car manufacturing.

Cars for all

The Ford Motor Company was the creation of Henry Ford, a largely self-taught mechanic. His forceful personality dominated the company for more than 40 years. He sometimes made mistakes, but he was usually clear in his own mind

about the direction in which the company should be moving.

The Ford Motor Company was set up soon after the first motor cars had been invented. At that time, cars were still expensive luxury items. Only wealthy people could afford to buy and run them. Henry Ford wanted to make a cheap, reliable car at a price ordinary people could afford.

Other car makers thought he was crazy. "You can make more money by selling expensive cars," they said. But Ford knew that if only the rich could buy cars, the motor industry would never grow. In spite of false starts, he pursued his aim of making cars that many people could afford. And his work helped to change the idea of personal transportation forever.

◀ In the early twentieth century only the rich could afford cars. Roads were nothing more than rough dirt tracks. When it rained cars would get stuck in the mud and passers-by shouted "Get a horse!" to the unlucky motorists.

9

The man behind the motor

Henry Ford was born and brought up on a farm at Dearborn, Michigan, USA. Henry was always fascinated by machines. As a boy, he loved taking things apart to see how they worked – particularly toys and watches.

► Young Henry loved helping his father on the family farm. When he was a boy, motorized tractors had not been invented.

▼ The first Ford car was little more than a box on wheels. It had a single seat, a tiller to steer with, and an electric bell to warn the unwary of its approach.

From steam engines to cars

When Henry was 12 years old, he got his first sight of a steam engine moving along the road under its own power. The experience fired his ambition to become an engineer. Four years later he became an apprentice at a machine shop in Detroit, learning his trade while earning his living. At 19 he became a travelling repairman for a firm that made portable steam engines. He stayed in this job for ten years, learning all the time, then went to work for a Detroit electric light company as its chief engineer.

The car had just been invented in Europe, and cars soon captured the imagination of Henry Ford. In 1896 he built his first car. He called it the Quadricycle, because it had four bicycle wheels linked by a frame. It was much lighter and faster than other "horseless carriages" of the time and greatly impressed the mayor of Detroit, William Maybury. He provided the money for Ford to build a second, better car.

Detroit Automobile Company

Ford's second car attracted the attention of a rich Detroit businessman, William H. Murphy. Murphy took it for a trial run of 100 kilometers (60 miles) and was pleased to find that it didn't break down. On the strength of this trial, Murphy, Maybury and others set up the Detroit Automobile Company in 1899. Ford became its mechanical superintendent.

Ford had a lot to learn about business. He spent too much time making design improvements and not enough on actually building the car for sale. He kept saying his design was not ready. And in just over a year the Detroit Automobile Company closed.

Success and failure

Ford now turned his attention to designing racing cars. In a race in Detroit in 1901, he easily beat the leading American car maker Alexander Winton. Murphy and four others who had lost money in the Detroit Automobile Company became interested again. They formed the Henry Ford Company to build another car to Ford's design. But once again, Ford failed to put his car into production quickly enough. And in 1902, after only four months, Murphy and his partners fired him. They went on to build the car Ford had designed, and changed the name of the business to the Cadillac Automobile Company. As the Cadillac, Henry Ford's car was a great success. But Ford himself had failed twice in business.

▲ Henry Ford stands with his first car in front of his Detroit workshop, overlooked by a man and beast whose services it was destined to usurp.

BUSINESS MATTERS: HARD WORK

Henry Ford built his first car in his spare time. He worked until nearly midnight every evening in a small workshop at the back of his home. "No work with interest is ever hard," he said years later. Ford was a hard worker all his life and was rewarded with business success.

Most successful people will agree that there is no substitute for hard work. Those at the top of an organization often work the longest hours, getting up early and finishing late at night.

Third time lucky

▲ The first Ford factory in Detroit quickly became too small. By April 1904 the company had 300 employees.

▼ Barney Oldfield, a novice driver, put his foot down and took Ford's 999 car to victory at Grosse Pointe, Michigan, in 1902. This painting of the event is by HC McBarron.

After Ford left the Henry Ford Company in 1902, he worked for a while with another Detroit businessman, Tom Cooper. Cooper provided Ford with the money to build racing cars. This time Ford worked with a skilled engineer, C. Harold Wills, who made accurate working drawings from Ford's sketches. The result was the powerful racer, the 999. It soon won an important race and set a new American speed record.

The Ford Motor Company

In 1903 Henry Ford was ready to learn from his earlier mistakes. This time he was interested in building an ordinary car, and he had a straightforward design with a new engine already prepared. He teamed up with a well-to-do coal merchant, Alex Y. Malcolmson, who wanted to invest money in the growing automobile business. He and a group of other tradesmen put up $28,000 as capital for the new company. It was called the Ford Motor Company.

The business side of the project was handled by one of

Malcolmson's employees, James Couzens. Couzens kept tight control over the company's affairs and made up for his employers' lack of business knowledge.

Ford on the road

Ford called his new car the Model A. The new company did not actually make the car; they provided the design and brought in ready-made parts. All that happened in Ford's workshop was assembly – putting the parts together. Couzens reckoned that once all the costs of production had been paid for, they could sell the cars for $750 and make a profit of $150 on each one.

But it was not that easy. Production began in June 1903. For the first four weeks the Ford Motor Company was paying out money. And there was nothing coming in except what the investors had contributed. The company had what every business dreads: a cash flow problem.

Then came Ford's first sale. It was not just for a standard Model A, but a four-seater version costing $100 more. In the next eight months the Ford Motor Company sold 658 cars.

▲ The upholstered seat behind the front bench seat on this Model A was an optional extra that turned the car into a four- rather than a two-seater.

Popular or luxury cars?

In the early years of motoring cars were hand-built by crafts-men, using parts that were made to fit only one car. Cars were luxury items. They cost a lot to produce and were expensive to buy. Manufacturers sold only a few. But they made a big profit on each car.

Henry Ford belonged to a group of pioneer car makers who believed that cars should be made in larger numbers and sold to anybody who wanted to buy them, rich and poor alike. Ford genuinely believed that the motor car as a means of personal transportation should be available to everyone.

▶ This photograph of Henry Ford with his son Edsel in a Model F was taken in about 1905.

Boardroom battle

In 1904 Ford offered the public three different cars – the two-cylinder Model C at $800, the Model F at $1,000 and the four-cylinder Model B at $2,000. Model B did not sell well and was dropped. But Malcolmson wanted the firm to increase production of an even more expensive car – the six-cylinder Model K. Henry Ford, however, had already decided that his future lay in selling cheaper cars by the million.

In the boardroom battle that followed, Malcolmson left the company. Ford bought out Malcolmson's share of the business, and the shares of some other partners too. Even so, he still owned only 58% of the business.

◀ Henry Ford at the wheel of a Model K. Behind him sits James Couzens, the man whose sound business sense helped Henry to success.

Having decided to build affordable cars for as wide a market as possible, Ford made the Model N. It went on sale at $600. The company dropped all its other models to concentrate on this tough four-cylinder car. And the company made a profit of more than a million dollars in a single year. It went on to produce Models R and S, which were luxury versions of the Model N.

BUSINESS MATTERS: STOCKS AND SHARES

Some companies are privately owned by an individual, a family or a group of investors. Others are publicly owned. Shares in the company can be bought or sold on the stock market. Shares are what they sound like – a share in the company. Together the shares are called stock. Selling stocks and shares in your business is a good way to raise money for expansion. But it also means giving away some control of the business. The people who run the company become answerable to the shareholders. Each year they must declare a dividend, a share of the profit to be divided up among the shareholders as a return on the money they have invested. If the company does badly, there will be no dividend for the shareholders and they may decide to sell their shares. This makes the price of the shares drop and reduces the value of the company.

◀ This model K, lovingly restored by its owner, is a grand car – too grand for the ordinary millions whom Ford wanted to see on wheels.

A car for the multitude

These models were all just practice for Ford's next car, the Model T. This was designed in secret by Ford in a locked room at the top of his factory. It was the people's car he had been dreaming of. Henry Ford announced its launch with the ringing words, "I will build a car for the multitude."

A revolutionary car

The Model T had some striking new features. Until this time, the cylinders for car engines were made separately and bolted together. Ford designed an engine with all four cylinders mounted on a single block, and a detachable top, or cylinder head. This made it easier to put the car together and easier to repair, too. Today all car engines are made this way.

Ford himself oversaw every detail of the new car. He aimed

1

2

3

4

16

to make it simple to drive and to look after. No special skill was needed to take it apart. Cheap spare parts could be bought at hardware shops; the owner need never hire a mechanic. The Model T was well made, light in weight and very strong. It could cope with the rough roads and tracks of the countryside. At last, here was a car that many ordinary families could afford. The Model T went on sale in October 1908 at $850 and in only one color – black. It was an instant success.

The Tin Lizzie

In 1909 Henry Ford turned over the company's complete production to Model Ts. Between 1908 and 1927 more than 15 million Model Ts were sold in the United States, nearly 1 million in Canada, and 300,000 in Britain. It was probably the most successful car ever built. Its owners gave it the affectionate name "Tin Lizzie."

▲ Black paint dried more quickly than colored paint, so Henry Ford preferred orders for black Model Ts.

1 The Model T was cheap enough for ordinary people to buy, but not all its buyers were ordinary. This car and owner clearly went through a lot together.
2 An Indian maharajah's Model T, fully equipped for hunting.
3 & 4 The Model T was adapted as a truck and as a stylish bus.
5 The Model T was responsible for America's first traffic jams.
6 This cover illustration from the August 1916 edition of the *Ford Times*, shows that even the countryside was not free of traffic.

On the line

The speedy and efficient production of a huge number of cars allowed Ford to make large profits. At first every Ford car was hand-built, using parts supplied by other firms. The cars were built in a series of operations, being wheeled from one worker to another as each stage of work was finished. The string of workers and operations was called an assembly line. This method of car production had first been used by Detroit car maker Ransom E. Olds, inventor of the Oldsmobile, in the early 1900s.

In 1908 the cost of a Model T was $850 – too expensive for many people. Henry Ford knew that, to get the price down, he would have to cut production costs. He looked hard at his factory. How could he improve things?

Moving along

As a first step, he decided that the company could make a lot of the parts itself, to save buying them at a higher price. The parts were made so accurately that they needed no adjustment before being fitted. And they were interchangeable, each part neatly fitting into place in any car of the same model.

Henry Ford could see two main problems in the way his men were working. First, there was too much walking about the factory to collect parts and tools. Second, each man had too many jobs to do. Both problems were solved by the

► Early conveyor belt production at Ford's Highland Park factory. Each person adds or tightens a different component as flywheels move along the waist-high shelf.

18

development of a moving assembly line. Under the new system, the frame of each car moved along the floor of the factory on a chain. Parts moved on a parallel conveyor belt. As the frame came opposite each worker, he did one or two simple tasks only. Then he did exactly the same to the next car, and the next. As Ford put it, "The man who puts in a bolt does not put on the nut; the man who puts on the nut does not tighten it." Each simple job could be done by an unskilled or semi-skilled worker, so fewer skilled workers were needed. Time was saved at each stage.

Cutting time cuts costs

Before the improvements, it had taken twelve and a half hours to build the Model T. In 1914 it took just over one and a half hours. This big saving in time cut Ford's production costs. In 1916, the Model T was selling at less than $400. And as Ford further reduced the cost of making a car, its selling price dropped. By 1925, Henry Ford was able to sell the Model T at only $260.

▲ Only things moved in Ford's factories. People stood still and let the parts come to them. Here upholstered seating units slide down from the first floor and fit neatly on to chassis rolling out from the ground floor.

▼ Today the people are mostly gone. Robots, like these welders, have taken their place.

Competition

Ford continued to make large profits throughout the early 1920s. The company made enough to build its massive Rouge factory at Dearborn, to invest in its own coal and iron mines, and to set up its own steel and glass-making works. But by 1926 sales were steadily falling.

Market changes

Henry's son Edsel, now president of Ford, could see that the motorcar market was changing. People were no longer happy with the basic, black Model T. They wanted something more modern and comfortable. But Henry stood firm against any changes that would upset his production flow. Meanwhile, competitors such as General Motors began to produce cars with extra comforts. By 1929 Ford sales had fallen to $0.35 million while General Motors' sales were $1.6 million. Henry Ford at last agreed to a change.

▲ By the late 1920s the Model T was looking old-fashioned. People wanted a change.

► In 1927 Chevrolet sales outstripped Ford's for the first time. This Chevrolet ad claimed the car "Fits the Finest Homes or Most Modest Incomes." It appealed to the same market as the Model T but the car was cheaper, more comfortable and more up to date.

The Model A

The last Model T was made in 1927. Henry decided not to change his car, but instead to make a completely new one. After a five-month shut-down of assembly lines, the Model A appeared. It was the first car to have, as standard, safety glass in its windscreen. It came in a choice of four colors and 17 body

styles. At first the Model A was a great success. After one month, Ford was producing six thousand a day. But competitors were bringing out improved models each year. And after five years the Model A had gone out of style.

In 1932 Henry Ford introduced the V–8, the first low-priced car with an eight-cylinder engine. It came in a range of colors, was very quiet, and could travel at nearly 130 km/h (80 mph). Despite these later models, Ford never regained its number one place. Henry Ford had shown himself to be more interested in production processes than in what the customer wanted.

▲ The Model A was launched in late 1927. For a year it outsold the Chevrolet, but then the Chevrolet rode past it again.

BUSINESS MATTERS: INNOVATION

Keeping up with changes in technology and keeping ahead of your rivals is vital in business. Everybody wants the latest thing. Businesses that are content with a successful product are always in danger. Sooner or later somebody will think of something better and, if the business is not ready, willing and able to adapt, it will be overtaken. Making changes, however, brings problems in the workplace because few people enjoy change. They like the familiar and fear the unknown. Helping workers adapt to new conditions and learn new skills is as important as installing the new high-tech equipment in the factory.

▶ The 1932 V8 engine was an innovation, but so was the depression that slowed sales throughout the 1930s.

INTRODUCING THE NEW FORD V·8
WITH CENTRE-POISE
NEW RIDING COMFORT

ALL PASSENGERS RIDE BETWEEN THE AXLES

Working at Ford

The assembly line system allowed Ford to produce more and more cars. But it was boring, repetitive work, and so people moved on. It cost the company $100 to train each new worker. And in 1913 accountants worked out that Ford was losing millions of dollars a year in staff training. Couzens and Henry Ford wondered how they could make people stay. Couzens came up with the idea of raising pay to five dollars a day. This was double what most wage earners received. Henry Ford agreed. The news rocked the nation, and workers flocked to the Ford factory.

Labor relations

Over the years, labor relations were often difficult. In 1927 the firm laid off workers while changing from the Model T to new models. Workers who had been with Ford for a long time expected their jobs back when production started again. But there were no guarantees.

Depression

During the 1930s, America and Europe were in the grip of a deep depression. Nobody was buying new cars. Unemployment rocketed as businesses lost customers and closed. In 1932 Ford cut daily wages to $4, below the standard rate for the job. Calls for labor unions at Ford were met with violence, some of which Henry Ford allowed. Ford hated unions and resisted them as long as he could. But in 1941 he was persuaded to sign an agreement with the union. From then on

▲ Multilingual employees answer customers' calls at Ford Credit. Today there are few unskilled jobs. Ford trains its employees but most still need basic skills to get a job.

BUSINESS MATTERS: HUMAN RESOURCES

The people who work for a company are its most important assets. They are often called human resources, and no company can survive without them. Firms keep their staff by paying competitive wages and offering attractive benefits. In an age of automation and computer control, there is less demand for unskilled workers. So people with the wrong type of skill or no skill at all can find it hard to get a job.

▶ Meals are provided for hungry factory and office workers at Ford's Dagenham plant in the UK.

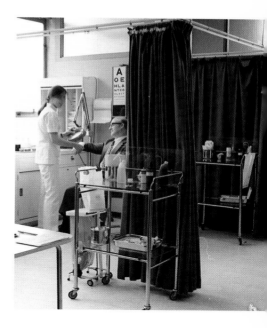

the Union of Automotive Workers (UAW) represented Ford employees in the United States.

Today, Ford has generally good relations with its workforce. It is an equal opportunity employer. The company works together with the UAW and other national unions to plan training programmes for employees. But occasionally there are strikes over pay and working conditions.

▲ Ford offers its staff regular medical check-ups, and medical staff are always available to give emergency aid and advice on health matters.

◀ A team of Canadian Customer Assistance staff and managers brainstorm ideas to improve customer service.

Education and training

Like all big firms, Ford spends quite a lot of money on teaching workers the skills they need to do their jobs. Before starting work on the assembly line, employees get between 80 and 120 hours of training. They learn about the vehicle's construction and special features. Nearly all Ford factories have an education or "open learning" center where staff can learn using the latest computers and interactive videos. Courses teach employees to work together as teams.

How Ford manages

Henry Ford liked to do things his own way and would not listen to his investors. They even took him to court on a charge of business mismanagement and won. Undeterred, Henry bought back their shares so that he could continue to control his company.

Family firm

In 1919 Edsel Bryant Ford, Henry's only son, became president of the company, but as chairman of the board Henry still had the power.

In 1920 the company was reorganized, with all the shares owned by the Ford family. In 1936 Henry Ford and Edsel set up a charitable fund called the Ford Foundation. After Edsel's death in an accident in 1943 and Henry's death in 1947, 90 per cent of the shares were owned by the Ford Foundation. But Edsel's sons still controlled the company. They owned the only shares that carried the right to vote on the board of directors.

Public company

In 1956 the Ford Foundation sold its shares to the public. From then on Ford became a public company, though for a

▼ The 1994 board of directors with the new Ford world car vehicle family. Most of the board are non-executive directors who run other important US businesses.

time the family still controlled the running of the business. Today it operates like other large companies, with executives responsible to the board of directors, and the board answerable to the shareholders.

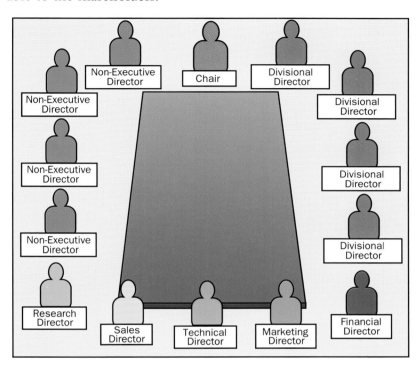

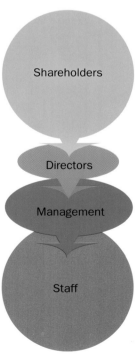

▲ A typical board of directors of a large company. In smaller companies, directors may have more than one role. In very small companies there may be only one director.

▶ The board of directors is answerable to the shareholders. The management and staff are answerable to the board.

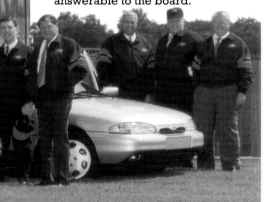

Selling Ford cars

Henry Ford himself made cars such as the Model T attractive because of the low prices he was able to charge. It was his business manager James Couzens who put the selling of Ford cars on a sound basis, beginning with the Model A back in 1903. Couzens, who worked with Ford until 1915, was faced with creating a means by which Ford cars could be distributed. He did it by setting up a network of dealerships.

Dealerships

There were no regular car dealers when Ford went into business. People who already sold other things, such as farm machinery or bicycles, became car salesmen. So did country

▲ Selling a Model A in 1931. Distribution is vitally important in any business. It is no use creating a product unless you can get it to potential customers.

JAMES COUZENS, 1872-1936

James Couzens was born in Canada in 1872. He became chief clerk and cashier to Alex Malcolmson and moved over to the Ford Motor Company when it started in 1903. He was largely responsible for its financial success. Couzens became business manager, treasurer and vice-president. In 1915 he resigned after an argument with Henry Ford.

▶ A comfortable showroom, with knowledgeable, helpful staff inspires confidence in the customer.

▶ Ford likes to keep its customers. One way is to give them speedy access to after-sales service rather than letting them go to competitors.

blacksmiths, who were the local engineers when it came to repairing machines.

Couzens had to organize this very mixed collection of people into a proper sales force. To make sure that the company did not suffer a cash flow problem, he had to be certain that each salesperson could afford to pay cash for the cars that the company supplied. In two years Couzens built up a force of 450 dealers scattered across America. Today Ford has 10,500 dealers all over the globe.

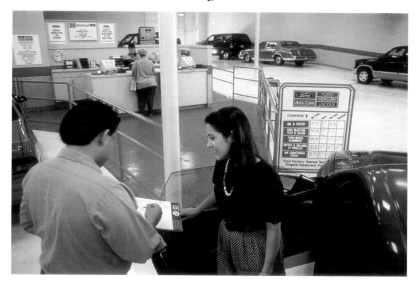

After-sales service

Couzens was also responsible for offering Ford customers a novel extra – an after-sales service. There was a team of factory-trained engineers ready to travel to help motorists keep their cars going. Today, Ford engineers still make routine and emergency service calls when needed. The Ford Auto Club provides a 24-hour emergency road and tow service.

From the thousands of Ford dealers worldwide, you can easily get spare parts for any car that is being made, and also for many older models too. In the United States, Ford provides a free telephone hotline for customers seeking help or advice from specially trained engineers. The Ford Customer Care Service has equipment that can report on the availability of replacement parts, work out repair costs and fix up a workshop appointment, all within seconds.

Ford customers can take their cars to their local dealer's service center for routine non-warranty work and repairs. This fosters brand loyalty, making customers more likely to replace their old Ford with a new one when the time comes.

Ford goes places

The Ford Motor Company began selling cars abroad right from the start. The first Ford cars seen in Europe were two Model As exported to Britain in 1903. In 1904 Ford set up its first foreign offshoot company, the Ford Motor Company of Canada. In the same year it set up a sales organization in London. Its first British assembly plant, in Manchester, followed in 1911.

Ford of Europe, formed in 1966, made cars for sale in Europe and elsewhere. More than 1,500,000 cars, commercial vehicles and tractors were produced a year. The vehicles were specially designed to suit the demands and tastes of European customers.

▲ The giant Saarlouis plant in south-west Germany opened in 1968 and began producing cars for France and Italy as well as Germany.

▲ The Ford Transit and the Fiesta have long been bestsellers in Europe but they are not available in America. The Mondeo is Europe's version of Ford's world car which is available in North America as the Ford Contour and Mercury Mystique.

Multinational Ford

Ford's international operation covers over 100 countries. Until 1994 it was organized into five groups: North America, South America, Europe, Asia-Pacific and Africa. Then it was decided to re-merge all the groups, starting with Europe and North America.

This will save the duplication of resources, human and material. Instead of building separate assembly-lines for small-engined cars each side of the Atlantic, now there will be only one. Under-the-skin components will be the same but the look and feel of the cars will be made to suit individual markets and local tastes.

BUSINESS MATTERS: MULTINATIONAL COMPANIES

Multinational companies are large businesses that operate in several different countries. With more than 300,000 employees working in 26 countries and serving customers in more than 200 countries, Ford is the world's fourth biggest multinational company. Multinationals have enormous economic power. By basing production in other countries, they are often able to control the supply of the resources they need and benefit from the lower costs of local labor and raw materials. They are also able to avoid import taxes and high distribution costs. If they are to employ lots of local people, some governments grant special tax concessions to encourage them to stay.

Global Ford

This global approach to managing the business has been made possible by the availability of new technology, including telecommunications, advanced computers and satellite television. It enables Ford to work as a team around the world, and to target specific markets.

Ford's traditional markets are not growing as quickly as those of the newly developed countries, where the demand for new vehicles is growing steadily. So the company is working to increase sales in Asia, India, South America and other developing countries, including Vietnam.

▲ A police officer in northern Norway relies on his Ford Mondeo, supplied by the company's northernmost dealer. The car is specially equipped to cope with temperatures as low as –50° Celsius.

▼ Like other car manufacturers, Ford is anxious to do well in the fast-expanding Chinese market, where its competitors are already making an impact.

Fighting on new fronts

With slow car sales throughout the 1930s, Ford went further into decline. From being the number one auto manufacturer controlling two-thirds of the market, the company slid to near bankruptcy in the 1940s.

When Edsel died in 1943, Henry became president again. By now he was old and tired and his judgement was not always sound. He left a lot of the business affairs to incompetent employees. This was a hectic time for Ford. The United States had entered World War II and the company was putting its whole production into the war effort. At last, in 1945, two years before his death, Henry Ford handed control over to his grandson, Henry Ford II.

Reorganization

Henry Ford II found that the company was badly run down and no match for its rivals General Motors and Chrysler. In fact, Ford was losing $9 million a month. Young Henry reorganized the company and brought in new talent. He employed ten former Air Force officers, known as the Whiz Kids, to work on the restructuring. They brought modern management techniques to Ford along with strong financial abilities. Eventually, the company was prosperous again.

One of Ford's major assets at this time was a brilliant young designer called Lido Iacocca, known as Lee. He joined the company in 1946, and in 1964 his team produced the design for the Ford Mustang which sold in millions.

▶ The European motor industry took off after World War II. The small, economical Volkswagen "Beetle" became the bestselling car of all time. It and other European cars found many customers in the United States who realized that small cars were more sensible.

FORD'S BIG FLOP

In 1957 Ford launched a car to fill the gap between its cheap and expensive models. The Edsel was a fine, medium-priced car, with futuristic styling, but nobody wanted it. The public did not like its high vertical radiator grill. They were used to wide, smiling grills, and the general boom in car sales that had made Ford executives rush the car on to the market had slowed. People preferred cheaper cars. Production stopped in 1959, by which time the Edsel had lost Ford $250 million.

ROBERT STRANGE McNAMARA, 1916-

Robert McNamara joined Ford in 1946 as one of the Whiz Kids who helped put the company back on its feet. McNamara introduced strict accounting methods and encouraged the company to develop both compact and luxury car models. In 1960 he was made president of Ford but soon left to become Secretary of Defense under President John Kennedy. Later, he headed the World Bank.

▶ Sales of the sleek Chrysler New Yorker outstripped those of the Edsel.

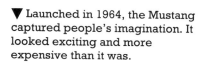

▼ Launched in 1964, the Mustang captured people's imagination. It looked exciting and more expensive than it was.

▼ The Associates is one of three units that make up Ford Financial Services Group. It owns the Amoco Oil Company's gasoline discount card and its credit card. Profits from financial services are more dependable than profits from the auto industry, which is more sensitive to recession and boom.

► The Japanese branch of The Associates is the largest foreign-owned finance company in the country. It acts like a bank, providing credit and other financial services.

Branching out

No business can afford to stand still. Businesses need to grow and expand. They can increase their profits by selling more and reducing costs. Efficient businesses strive to make savings and attract new customers all the time.

Immediately after World War II, when Henry Ford II took over the business, the Ford Motor Company began to look for ways in which it could expand. The end of the war brought hard times for a company already in decline, as car sales took a long time to recover.

Henry Ford II found part of the answer to his problem in a limited form of diversification. Diversification is the process of developing new products or markets in order to spread the burden of risk, take advantage of spare resources, or enlarge the business. For Ford the main aim was to spread the risk.

New directions

During the war Ford made armaments and military vehicles. In the 1950s, through the influence of the Whiz Kids, it set up a company to develop and manufacture weapons systems and produce missiles. Later it bought up the Philco Corporation in order to make electronic goods.

BUSINESS MATTERS: LEASING

When you lease something, you do not actually own it, though it is yours to use. At the end of a certain period, you (the lessee) must return it to the lessor (the owner), or pay extra money to buy it. Today, many businesses lease rather than buy cars and other equipment that they need. They have the benefit of the equipment but do not need to pay for it all at once or keep it forever. The lessor makes money because the payments work out at more than the cost of the equipment.

▶ Ford Credit also operates in Japan, providing finance for Japanese Ford dealers and their customers. In the US it finances nearly one-third of all Ford's sales.

▲ Red Carpet Leasing is part of US Leasing, the third unit of the Financial Services Group. It organizes and finances leases of all manner of equipment from cars to computers to commercial jet aircraft.

Moving into money

A more important and profitable form of diversification for Ford came in the 1980s. Through its company Ford Credit, Ford was already arranging loans and motor insurance for buyers of Ford cars. In 1985 the company bought First Nationwide Bank, a savings and loan institution. This was followed in 1987 by the purchase of US Leasing, which handles leasing arrangements on items as different as office computer systems and jet airplanes. In 1989 Ford bought The Associates, a finance company that also issues credit cards. Together, these companies make up the Financial Services Group.

The wisdom of these purchases became clear as the car market slid into recession in the early 1990s. At the end of 1991 the Financial Services Group made a profit of $927.5 million, the only sector of Ford to turn a profit that year.

Everything we do is driven by you.

▲ Ford's determination to please its customers paid off with the Fiesta, one of its most successful cars in Europe.

Customer is king

"Everything we do is driven by you," says a Ford slogan. Ford is committed to its customers. In such a highly competitive industry, the company realizes the importance of finding out what the public wants, and meeting those demands.

Safety and security

Safety and security have now become major considerations for car buyers. Today's cars offer safety features that were either unheard of fifteen years ago, or available only on the most expensive models. Safety testing standards are different across the world, so Ford has adopted its own company safety guidelines, the Dynamic Safety Engineering Strategy. Its cars have a specially strengthened bodyshell with impact bars to protect against side collisions, and a steering-wheel airbag.

Security became an important issue in the early 1990s, due to rising car theft and "joy riding." Ford, like other car manufacturers, has improved security on all its vehicles. It now

▶ A final inspector examines new Lincoln Continentals. Modern computerized production processes leave little room for errors.

▲ A robot dummy tests the steering-wheel airbag, a safety feature standard on all new Ford cars.

offers central locking, alarms and a special immobilizer system that prevents a car from moving until it receives a coded signal.

Comfort and color

People are spending longer and longer in their cars, so it is essential for car manufacturers to make vehicles more comfortable for both driver and passenger. Advances in electronics have made dashboards more informative, with push-button controls and more automatic features. Customers can choose the fabrics for their seats, the headlinings and floor coverings, as well as the paintwork color inside and out. The range available is based on customer research and studies of trends in shops, magazines and fashion houses. Durability is also important. Laboratory tests ensure that new fabrics are strong, hardwearing and stain resistant.

BUSINESS MATTERS: MARKET RESEARCH

Henry Ford worked at a time when business executives used their knowledge and experience to guess how big a demand for a product or service was likely to be without actually surveying people's needs and tastes. Formal market research started only in the 1920s in Germany. Today few firms would launch a new product without commissioning surveys of consumer demands and preferences, making sales forecasts, or testing an experimental version of the product. Ford is no exception.

FIESTA FINDINGS

An extensive market research program was carried out when designing the Fiesta in the early 1970s. Several prototype cars were made and at product clinics Ford asked over 5,000 members of the public what they wanted in a small car. Interviewers called on people in their homes, too, to find out their opinions on body style, engine size, mechanical features and extras. Over three years, all the findings from this research were put together. The result was the compact, value-for-money Fiesta which first appeared in 1976, and has been popular ever since.

▶ The message is simple. Forget the bus, you can afford a Ford!

▼ Nothing succeeds like success. Winning races and rallies gives Ford a glamorous image.

Advertising

The advertising of Ford cars has changed dramatically since the time of Henry Ford. In the early 1900s, advertising meant selling in print or through publicity events such as races. Today advertising means selling on television and radio, as well, and giving the company's name and products as much exposure as possible in newspapers and public events.

In the early days, when motorcars were seen by many as new-fangled pieces of machinery, Ford decided to demonstrate their durability. In 1911 a Model T climbed Ben Nevis, the highest mountain in Britain. In 1912 a Model T was the winner in a scramble up Mount Wilson in California.

By 1914 the Ford Motor Company was producing almost half of America's cars. Ford had established itself as "The Friend of the Family." Advertisements showed parents and children using a Ford for outings. Economy was often a key selling point. In the 1950s, the Ford Popular was billed as the "Lowest priced car in the world."

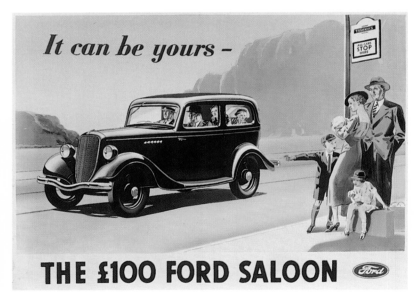

Creating a campaign

Today Ford employs advertising agencies to produce sophisticated campaigns for television and radio, for newspapers and magazines, and for billboards along the highway and on public transportation. Like the cars, the basic material is the same, but local markets can modify advertisements to suit their own particular needs.

Development of the campaign for the Mondeo started two years before the car was launched. Its target market was identified and research was done to produce the most effective method of advertising. "Beauty with inner strength" was its initial slogan, designed to put across the message that the car was safe, secure and environmentally friendly.

Auto racing

Ford's involvement in auto racing is as old as the company itself. Henry Ford realized that the quickest way to gain publicity was to win a race. The company's backing of the Benetton-Ford Grand Prix team kept it in the eye of car-racing enthusiasts round the world and gave it an exciting, youthful image.

BUSINESS MATTERS: TRADEMARKS

A trademark is a name, design or symbol that helps a customer identify a company's products. Trademarks that are registered are legally protected to prevent copying by a rival company. Only Ford cars can carry the Ford trademark.

◀ Once it was standard practice for motor manufacturers to drape beautiful model girls over their cars. But even in the early 1970s, when this shot was taken, women were objecting to being exploited in this way.

◀ Modern ads sell you the car. One agency produces a basic campaign, and individual countries (here, Sweden and Norway) adapt the material to best suit their market.

Technology and design

Technology has given car manufacturers new tools. Today, designers use computers to help them work out the shapes and styles of future models. Every major project is handled by a design team. The team follows the car throughout its development and continues to monitor its progress even after it has left the production line.

The new technology has also enabled Ford to cut costs, save time, and improve quality and productivity. One production team found a way to reduce the time it takes to develop a new engine prototype from more than a year to 100 days.

Realizing the importance of innovation, the company has increased its investment in research and design, and opened new research centers in Europe and Japan. The engine for three of Ford's latest cars (the Contour, the Mondeo and the Mercury) was the result of a global research program made possible by modern communications systems.

▲ Ford has the most up-to-date computers available. This electronic simulation of a car has just hit a wall at 31mph.

▲ Ford engineers have developed a technique using this device to develop an engine prototype in 100 days, a job that formerly took a year or more.

◄ This award-winning 24-valve engine was developed for the "world car" by a team of engineers from Britain, Germany and the United States. It is compact, lightweight and can run for 100,000 miles between tune-ups.

38

THE LOOK

Ford learned an important business lesson in the 1920s with the Model T. A car design can never be allowed to stay the same for long. The style of a car is as important as its engine.

The Lincoln Continental

The 1930s brought a more streamlined look to car design. The head of Ford's design department at this time was Eugene T. Gregoire. With Edsel Ford, he created the Lincoln Continental, voted one of the ten best-styled cars of all time by the New York Metropolitan Museum of Art.

▼ Lincoln Continental

▲ Ford is constantly trying to reduce harmful emissions from its cars. Here a test is carried out to find the effect of cold air on a Mondeo's exhaust fumes.

The Thunderbird

When the new American models appeared after World War II, the cars were sleek and showy. Ford's 1956 Thunderbird was a new car for a post-war generation.

▼ Thunderbird

▼ Cortina

The Cortina

In Britain in the 1960s, Ford's Cortina became the best-selling model. It was a light, roomy, medium-sized car, ideal both for families and for business people. Beginning with the 1962 models, the Cortina range was steadily developed over the years, becoming more comfortable and sophisticated to keep up with the public's demands.

▲ Ford uses recycled plastic covers to protect the seats of its new cars. This prevents large amounts of plastic being thrown on dumps.

▶ A choir of employees from The Associates in Dallas, Texas, helps the Salvation Army begin a campaign. The Associates staff are supporters of United Way and other charities.

▼ Barges on the River Danube carry new cars to Austria from Germany. It's a good way of reducing traffic and saving fuel.

Ford in the community

Like many large business organizations, the Ford Motor Company devotes part of its income to charities. It supports a wide range of educational, environmental, social and cultural projects. The company seeks to be a "good corporate neighbor" wherever it is in the world.

Community care

Every year Ford makes donations worth many millions of dollars to a number of civic, health, medical research and welfare programs and to activities in the areas of education, international relations and the arts. It sponsors sporting, conservation and arts activities.

Some projects take Ford employees directly into the community. In one project a senior Ford manager is lent to a school or college as industrialist-in-residence. The manager's task is to promote students' understanding of business and industry.

The environment

Preserving the environment is one of Ford's stated aims as a manufacturer. It funds education programs to help raise children's understanding of science. And in some cities it helps to send secondary-school pupils on environmental trips.

In its manufacturing processes, the Ford company is seeking to cut waste and to use and make goods that are recycled and recyclable. In one assembly plant in Michigan, all the

THE FORD FOUNDATION

Henry Ford and his son Edsel set up the Ford Foundation in 1936, as part of a reorganization of the company's financial structure. The Foundation is now an American institution and the world's largest charity. The Foundation grants money to many causes, including education, the relief of poverty and famine and the safeguarding of human rights. It has also helped set up communications and public-service television broadcasting, arts projects and environmental programs.

By 1995 the Foundation had given away more than $7 billion. The Foundation sold its shares in Ford in 1956. Today it has no connection with the company or the Ford family, but its good work continues under the supervision of a board of trustees.

▲ School students learn about aerodynamics from their industrialist-in-residence, an experienced Ford engineer on loan to the school.

BUSINESS MATTERS: TAX AND CHARITY

Every individual and every business that earns sufficient money must pay tax by law. Governments impose taxes in order to help pay for things for which they are responsible: defense, education, the police force, and so on. Most individual earnings are subject to income tax, company earnings to corporation tax. Accumulated wealth – savings and property – is subject to inheritance tax, often called death duties. In most countries companies gain some tax advantages by donating money to charity. By doing this, they are able to keep or use more of their profits than they otherwise could. This encourages them to continue giving to charity and it gives the company a good name with the public. It was to avoid paying a newly imposed inheritance tax that Henry Ford I and Edsel set up the Ford Foundation.

packaging in which components arrive is recycled instead of being dumped. About 75 per cent of a typical motor vehicle consists of materials that can be reused. Ford is studying ways of recycling whole cars.

The company is also seeking new ways to cut harmful lead and gas emissions – carbon monoxide, carbon dioxide and oxides of nitrogen – from exhaust pipes of Ford cars. All Ford gas–powered vehicles now have catalytic converters. These devices reduce pollution but they do not solve the real problem facing the world – the need for a car that can run efficiently on an alternative clean source of power.

▲ These children are enjoying EarthQuest, a Ford-sponsored interactive exhibit that helps children make everyday environment-friendly choices.

The road ahead

Ford sees its future in global terms. In 1994 the company made sweeping changes to its structure. More than 1,700 top Ford executives pledged their commitment to the goals of the company's reorganization by signing a "Wall of Commitment" at a global management meeting.

Towards 2000

The new organization, called Ford 2000, went into effect on January 1, 1995. The management structure was simplified, with more centralization – fewer layers of management – at the top of the company and less centralization lower down. In the past European plants produced cars for Europe, and North American plants produced cars for North America. Now each

▲ This experimental vehicle, named Synthesis 2010, is a test-bed on wheels, designed to reduce fuel use and emissions, and to be largely recyclable. It is made of lightweight aluminum.

▶ The 1996 Mercury Sable incorporates advanced new thinking in design and engineering.

▲ Car designs start as clay models. Then they are mocked-up to look like the real thing and become "concept" cars like this mini sportscar which Ford plans to produce for young buyers.

BUSINESS MATTERS: JOB SATISFACTION

Assemby line techniques are still used to some extent in the motor industry. Workers at many of Ford's plants put together cars from components sent from elsewhere. But the work can be boring and bring little satisfaction. New ways of working, with departments divided into teams, are being brought in. Each person in a team performs a variety of tasks and so the work is more satisfying. The team as a whole competes with other teams and takes pride in outperforming its rivals.

The shape of things to come for Europe's small car drivers. The Ka, seen here as a concept car, is already in production.

Ford has got the message that all businesses need to heed.

of five new vehicle production centers produces a range of cars or trucks that will sell to all markets.

People working in teams at the vehicle centers are empowered to make their own policies, innovations and decisions – as though they were in a small company. They can respond more quickly to the needs of individual customers, and produce and sell more cars.

Being the best

Ford's commitment is to be the world's leading motor company, to lead in quality, customer satisfaction, business practice, training and empowerment, and shareholder value. Environmental concerns will remain a top priority. Ford is part of a team of companies studying new ways to reduce the poisonous content of fuels. Development of more energy-efficient engines will continue, alongside Ford Ecostars, vans driven by electric motors and powered by batteries. Perhaps vehicles like these will be the Model Ts of the future.

Alex Trotman (left), chairman of Ford, and Ed Hagenlocker, president of Ford Automotive Operations, stand by the "Wall of Commitment." a pledge of support for the goals of the company's global reorganization, signed by all senior executives.

Create your own business

▲ Keep your project simple, and plan carefully. Planning will help you avoid mistakes.

Henry Ford built cars on an assembly line in order to give people a product they could afford. See if you can create and market a popular product at a price your customers can afford. See how mass production techniques work to produce it. Will you use an assembly line or a team?

The product
Think of a good idea for a product. Perhaps you could market a cassette tape of a concert by the school orchestra or rock band. Do some market research to see what people would like, how much they would pay and whether they would pay for the product in advance or

lend you money to get your business going. Before you start get permission from your school.

Management
You will need to select or elect a small team to manage the project. Each person should have a specific role, to look after the design, production, publicity, selling and so on.

Capital
If everyone involved contributes some of their own money, they may find parents willing to lend money. You must offer to return the money with a set amount of interest or a percentage of the profits.

Planning
Decide what you want to produce. If you decide on the rock concert, organize people to make the recording. You will probably be able to borrow or hire the equipment you need. Estimate the number of cassettes you can sell. What will be the maximum, what will be the minimum?

Costs
Work out how much it will cost you to record the music, buy blank cassettes, copy the cassettes, package them, advertise, publicize and distribute them. Remember the cost of your overhead, items like stationery, bus fares, and telephone calls.

PRODUCTION – LINE OR TEAM?

See if it is more effective to work on an assembly line or in a team. Try this experiment.

Method 1

Organize half your class into an assembly line. Arrange your desks so that the items you are putting together will flow smoothly from one stage to the next. Each person on the assembly line will carry out one task only, over and over again. Time yourselves to see how long it takes all the products to move through every stage of production.

Person 1: types and prints out the insert cards, saying who the artists are and what the music is.
Person 2: folds the cards and puts them in the cassette cases.
Person 3: packs each cassette into its case.
Person 4: types address labels.
Person 5: inserts the cassettes into packages for the mail.
Person 6: adds a piece of promotional literature about the school and its music.
Person 7: checks the packages' contents, seals and stamps them.
Person 8: takes the packages to the post office.

Method 2

Organize the remainder of your class into teams. Let each team put a number of the packages together. Get members to divide the tasks between them so that each person does more than one job.

Which way of working proves more efficient, and which more satisfying?

Work out the unit cost, the cost per item, by adding all the costs together and dividing them by the number you intend to produce. Work out the amount of money you hope to make from sales and divide it by the number of items. The difference between the two will be your profit per item.

Selling

Drum up publicity for your product. You should have advertised the cassette on the pre-concert publicity. Follow it up with ads in the school magazine and on notice boards. Ask local shops if they will take some cassettes to sell. See if you can get the local newspaper to run a story.

Accounts

Keep a record of what you spend and receive. Repay your investors and decide what to do with the profit. Will you give some or all of it to the school or to another charity? Will you spend it? Or will you reinvest it in a more ambitious project for the future?

▼ Proper businesses present their figures as a profit and loss account like this.

PROFIT AND LOSS ACCOUNT		
Sales		250.00
Less Cost of Sales		
Sound equipment	60.00	
Cassettes	10.00	
Inserts	10.00	
Design	10.00	
	90.00	(90.00)
Gross profit		160.00
Less Overhead		
Wages	10.00	
Stationery	5.00	
Telephone	5.00	
Bus fares	3.00	
	23.00	(23.00)
Net profit		137.00
Loan repayment	100.00	
Interest	10.00	
	110.00	(110.00)
Net profit after interest		27.00

The language of business

Accounting Keeping financial records that show money going into and out of a business.

Advertising Making publicly known. Advertisers use television, radio, newspapers and so on to tell everyone how good their product or service is.

Aerodynamics The science of flying and movements through air.

After-sales service Assistance and repairs available to customers for a certain time after the purchase of a product.

Aluminum Light silvery metal.

Apprentice Person who is bound to an employer and receives training and low pay in exchange for work.

Assembly line Series of machines and workers in a factory set up to assemble a product in a sequence of tasks.

Assets Anything owned by a business including property, money, goods and machines.

Automation Manufacture of a product using machines rather than people.

Bankruptcy Having no money in the bank or any means of paying debts.

Billion A thousand million or, in Britain, a million million. Billions in this book are a thousand million.

Board of directors See Directors.

Boom Time when business is good and customers can afford to buy products.

Brand The name of a company's product. See also Trademark.

Brand-loyalty The tendency of satisfied customers to buy more of a company's products.

Business An organization that sells goods or services in return for money.

Capital Money needed to start a business and keep it going.

Cash flow The rate at which money enters and leaves a business during any period of time.

Catalytic converter Device that reduces the amount of harmful substances emitted from a car's exhaust.

Chairman The person who leads a committee or board of directors. Also called a chairperson or chair.

Chassis Base frame of a car or other vehicle.

Chief executive The highest-ranking person in a company who has full power to act and make decisions on behalf of the company.

Choice Variety of products for customers to choose from.

Commercial To do with trade.

Company Organization of a group of people to carry on a business. Companies may be small or large, public or private. See also Corporation.

Competition The struggle for customers and profits between two or more enterprises in the same field.

Concept car Prototype of an innovative car.

Conveyor belt A continuously moving belt that transports goods, materials or packages during manufacture.

Corporation Business corporations are usually large, centrally organized public companies.

Costs The amount of capital that it takes to make and sell a product or service.

Credit To give credit is to allow time for a payment to be made.

Customer Anyone who buys from a seller, especially one who buys regularly.

Cylinder Chambers in an engine that contain the pistons that are driven up and down by exploding gasoline vapor. Most vehicles have four, six or eight cylinders.

Dealership Company licensed to sell another company's product.

Demand The amount of a product that people will buy.

Depression Extended period of recession.

Directors People who guide the activities of a company and make its most important decisions. They are members of the board of directors, which is led by the chairman or chief executive. The directors report to the managing director, who may also be the chairman of the board.

Distribution The means by which a product gets from the manufacturer to the customer.

Diversification The widening of the range of goods and services produced.

Dividend A small part of a company's profits paid to a shareholder in return for his or her investment.

Dollar Unit of US currency made up of 100 cents. The equivalent in UK pounds at the moment is about 66 pence, but rates of exchange between countries vary all the time.

Earnings Money gained by a person working or by a company selling.

Economy of scale A fall in the cost of production because of an increase in the size of a business.

Emission Waste gas from a car's exhaust.

Employee A person who works for another person or a company in return for a wage or salary.

Employer A person or company who provides work for employees.

Empowerment Giving people freedom to maximize their abilities and act for themselves.

Environment The surroundings in which people, animals and plants live.

Equal opportunity employer A company that hires staff on the basis of their qualifications, regardless of skin color, ethnic background, religion, sex, age, or disability.

Executive Director or senior manager of a company. See also Executive director.

Executive director A director who works for a company. A non-executive director is a member of the board but is not employed by the company. See also Directors.

Fiber-optic Transmission of light along filaments of glass.

Financial To do with money.

Financial director An executive responsible for financial planning, making and receiving payments, and keeping records.

Financial services Provision of loans, overdrafts, mortgages, purchase and leasing arrangements, and other forms of credit by banks, savings and loans, insurance companies, credit card companies and other institutions.

Firm Another name for a business.

Franchise A special agreement or license granted by a company (the franchisor) to a smaller business (the franchisee) allowing it to manufacture or sell goods or a service invented or owned by the franchisor.

Goods Things other than food produced by a business.

Gross See Net and gross.

Growth Expansion of a business to increase profits.

Human resources The people who work for a business. Also called staff or personnel.

Image How a company is seen by the public.

Import To bring goods into a country, or a good brought into the country.

Income The money that an individual or business receives from earnings or investments. Also called revenue.

Innovation The introduction of something new, such as a product, technique, technology or organizational structure.

Interest Money paid to investors for use of the money they have lent.

Invest To put money into a business or buy shares in it. The sum of money invested is called an investment.

Investor A person who invests.

Labor A collective name for workers, especially manual workers.

Leasing Credit arrangement whereby vehicles and equipment can be rented over a set period.

Liquidation The selling of a company's assets for cash.

Loss The money that a business loses when it spends more than it earns.

Manager A person who controls or organizes a business or part of it. A person who organizes a product.

Managing director See Directors.

Manufacturer A business that makes or produces goods.

Market The total number of buyers and sellers of a product.

Marketing All the activities involved in putting a product on the market, including research and development, distribution and sales, pricing and promotion.

Market research Surveying people's tastes and requirements to assess the demand for a product.

Mass market The majority of the population. Mostly low-priced products sell to the mass market.

Mission statement Summary of a company's aims and ambitions.

Net and gross A gross amount is money paid or earned before tax and other contributions have been deducted to leave a net amount.

Non-executive director See Executive director.

Overhead General costs, such as rent, heating, stationery and so on, that do not relate to a specific operation or item.

Physical resources Things such as buildings, machines and raw materials that a business uses.

Pioneer The first person to explore new territory or begin a new venture.

Pollution The spoiling of the environment by poisonous gases and other harmful substances.

Pressure group People who band together to exert influence on the government or other authority, or company, to change a law or policy.

Price The amount of money for which something can be bought or sold. Price is usually determined by supply and demand.

Private company A company that is owned by an individual or group of individuals, and whose shares are not traded on the stock exchange. See also Public company.

Product The thing that a business sells. Products can be goods or services.

Profit The difference between what a company earns – its income – and its costs.

Profit and loss account Part of the accounts that shows what profit or loss a company has made over a certain period.

Promotion 1 Moving up the employment scale to a better job. 2 Promoting sales by advertising, publicity and other sales incentives such as giveaway promotional items.

Prototype A trial model or first version of a product.

Public company A business that offers shares of itself for sale to the general public.

Publicity News or information about a company's activities and products.

Raw materials The ingredients needed to make a product.

Recession A time of unfavorable economic conditions when demand for goods is low.

Recycle To reuse materials rather than throwing them away.

Research Investigating new developments in design, technology and other fields. See also Market research.

Risk To invest money which may be lost.

Robot Device or mechanism that can replace humans in certain situations.

Salary Money paid in fixed amounts, usually monthly, to "white-collar" workers.

Sales force The "army" of people who are employed to sell a company's products.

Sales forecast Estimate of the likely number of sales to be made during a given period, based on experience and market conditions.

Service Providing help rather than goods.

Shareholder A person who owns shares in a company.

Shares Tiny portions of a company's capital value. The price at which shares are bought and sold goes up and down according to the company's success. See also Stock.

Sponsorship Providing money or other assistance for sporting, charitable or cultural events.

Staff All the people who work for a company, or workers other than the management.

Stock A block of shares.

Stock market Exchange where stocks and shares are bought and sold. Also called a stock exchange.

Streamlined Smoothly shaped so that wind or water flows easily over the surface of a moving object, allowing it to go faster.

Strike Refusal to work.

Tax Money that businesses and individuals have to pay the government from their earnings.

Technology The application of science to industry.

Trademark A name, design, symbol or some distinguishing mark that makes a company or product unique and recognizable. It is protected by law.

Trade union Associations formed by workers to improve their conditions and wages.

Trustee Person who holds property or money in trust for another and uses it to carry out their wishes.

Tune-up Adjustment of a car's engine to make it run as efficiently as possible.

Unemployment Lack of employment. Levels of unemployment rise during a recession.

Union See Trade union.

Wage Weekly payment of hourly rate paid to "blue-collar" (manual) workers.

Warranty Acceptance of responsibility for the quality and reliability of a product by the company that sells it for a specified term, during which free repairs will be carried out.

Welder Person or machine that fuses heated metals by beating.

Index

Numbers in *italics* indicate pictures and diagrams; those in **bold** indicate panel references.

A
Aerospace products 6
Advertising 36-37, *36-37*
  Chevrolet 20
After-sales service 27, *27*, **34**
Airbags 34, *35*
Alarms 35
Amoco Oil gasoline credit cards *32*
Armaments production 8, 18, 30
  diversification 32
Assembly line 18-19, *18-19*
  shut-down 20-21
Associates, The *32*, 33,*40*
Aston Martin (car company) **9**
Automotive Group **9**
Auto racing 36, *36*, 37

B
Benetton-Ford Grand Prix team 37
Bodyshell strengthening 34
Brand-loyalty 27, *27*
Britain, first Fords in 28
Business: creating your own 44-45
  language of 7, 46-47
  what it is 6-7

C
Cadillac Automobile Company 11, **18**
Capital **13**
  for Ford Motor Company 12
Cars: first Ford 10, *10*, **11**
  profit on *7*, 13
  see also individual models
Cash flow **13**
Central locking 35
Chairman *43*
  see also Ford, Henry
Charitable activities 24, 40-41
Chevrolet 20
Chrysler New Yorker *31*
Colors: customer research and 35
  for Model A 20-21
  for Model T 17, *17*
Company structure 25, *25*
Competition 20-21
  from small cars *30*
  new products and *6*
  sales *31*
Computers, use in design 38, *38*
Concept cars *42*, *43*
Contour car, engine for 38
Cooper, Tom 12
Cortina car *39*, *39*
Couzens, James 13, *15*, 26
  and after-sales service 27
  and sales force 27
Credit, giving *32*, 33
Credit companies *32*, 33, *33*
Customer Assistance staff *23*
Customer Care Service 27
Customers: Ford's commitment to 34-35, *34-35*
  hotline 27

D
Dagenham factory *22*
Dealerships 26-27, *26-27*
Dearborn Independent, The 8
Decision-making, employees and 43
Depression, economic 22-23
Design, importance of good **16**
Design team/designers 30
  and the look *39*, 39
  how they work 38, *38*, *42*
Detroit Automobile Company 11, *11*
Directors **25**
  board of 24, 25, *25*
Distribution costs 29
Dividend, declaring a 15
Durability 35, 36
Dynamic Safety Engineering Strategy 34

E
EarthQuest *41*
Ecostar vans 43
Edsel car **31**, *31*

Education: in the community 40-41, *41*
  staff programs 23
Electronic goods 6
Employees *6*
  and innovation 21
  benefits 22-23, *22-23*
  effect of mass production on 18-19, *18-19*
  job satisfaction *42*
  layoffs 22
  teams 42, 45
  turnover in 22
  union representation 23
  unskilled 22
  working conditions 22-23
Engines: development times 38, *38*
  electric 43
  for Model T 16
  four-cylinder 15
  future development 43
  industrial 6
  six-cylinder 14
  V-8 21, *21*
Environment: preserving the 40-41
  see also Pollution

F
Fabrics, laboratory testing 35
Factories: first *12*
  see also individual names
Farm machinery 6
Fiesta car 34
  market research on 35, *35*
Financial services 8
Financial Services Group **9**, *32*, 33, *33*
First Nationwide Bank 33
Fog Lamps, fiber-optic *6*
Ford, Edsel Bryant *14*, 20, 24
  eldest son 30, *30*
Ford, Henry 8, *8*, 10, *10 14*, *15*
  and marketing **34**
  and the unions 22-23
  apprenticeship 10
  business failures 10
  control of company 24
  Detroit workshop *10*
  philosophy 9
  secret design 16
  share of business 14
Ford 2000 42
Ford Credit 33, *33*
Ford Foundation 24, **41**
Ford II, Henry 30, *30*
Ford Motor Company **9**
  and the community 40-41
  as a public company 24-25
  as a family firm 24
  beginnings 12-13
  big flop 31, *31*
  boardroom battle 14
  company commitment 43, *43*
  decline and reorganization 30
  diversification 32-33, *32-33*
  first foreign offshoot 28
  international operations 28-29, *28-29*
  other businesses 8, 9, 20
  start of 9
  types of cars 14-15, *14-15*
  see also Company structure
Ford Motor Company of Canada 28
Ford of Europe, yearly production 28
Franchising/franchisees **27**

G
General Motors sales 20

H
Hagenlocker, Ed *43*
Henry Ford Company 11
Highland Park factory *18*
Human resources **22**
  buying *7*
  see also Employees

I
Iacocca, Lido (Lee) 30
Immobilizer system 35

Impact bars 34
Industrialist-in-residence 40, *41*
Inheritance tax 41
Innovation 21, *21*, 43
Investment 6, **13**
  in new factories 20
  in research and design 38

J
Jaguar (car company) **9**

K
Ka car *43*

L
Labor relations 22-23
Lagonda (car company) **9**
Leasing 33
Lincoln Continental car *34*, **39**, *39*
Loans 13

M
Malcolmson, Alex Y. 12
  buyout of 14
Management/managers 25
  job of 25
  simplification of structure 42-43
  trade unions and **23**
Managers **25**
Manchester factory 28
Market research **38**
Marketing **34**
Markets, finding a gap in **9**
Mass market **14**
Mass production 18-19, *18-19*
  see also Assembly line
Maybury, William 10
McNamara, Robert Strange **31**
Medical check-ups *23*
Mercury car, engine for 38
Mercury Sable car *42*
Model A car 13, *13*, 20-21, *21*
  exports 28
Model B car 14
Model C car 14
Model F car 14, *14*
Model K car 14, *15*
Model N car 15
Model T car 16-17, *16-17*, *20*
  build time 19
  cost of 18, 19
  durability tests 36
  replacement for 20
Mondeo car 29
  advertising campaign 37
  engine for 38
  exhaust tests 39
Money: uses of *7*
  see also Capital; Cash flow; Credit; Profits
Multinational companies **29**
Murphy, William H. 11
Mustang car 30, *31*

N
999 racing car 12, *12*

O
Oldfield, Barney *12*
Olds, Ransom E. 18
Open learning center 23

P
Parts: interchangeable 18
  ready-made 13
  see also Spare parts
People's car 16-17, *16-17*
Philco Corporation 32
Physical resources *6*, *7*
Policy: employees and 43
  on customers 26-27, *26-27*
Policy making 25
Pollution: publicity and 36
  testing exhaust emissions *39*
President 31, *43*
Product testing 34-35, *35*
Production: cutting costs 18
  wartime 8, 30
Products: the look of 39, *39*

experimental vehicles *42*
  launching 37
  range of products 6
  transportation of *40*
  types of 6
Profit: effect of mass production 18
  from financial services *32*, 33
  from Model N 15
  investment of 6, 20
  monthly losses 30
  what it is *7*
  see also Dividend
Publicity: public image and *36*, *36*
  racing and 37

Q
Quadricycle 10, *10*

R
Racing cars 11, 12, *12*
Recession **23**
  see also Depression, economic
Recycling: packaging 40, *40*
  scrap cars 41
Red Carpet Leasing 33
Roads *9*
Robots *19*
Rouge factory 20

S
Saarlouis factory 28
Safety features 34, *35*
Safety glass 20
Safety testing standards 34, *35*
Sales 26-27, *26-27*
  competitors 20, *20*
  economy and 36
  falling 20
  global market 29, *29*
  see also After-sales service; Dealerships; Market research
Security features 34-35
Service centers 27
Shareholders 25
  share in profits *see* Dividend
Showrooms *26*
Spare parts: for Model T 17
  obtaining 27
Stocks and shares 13, **15**
  buyback by Ford 24
  right to vote 24
Strikes 23
Synthesis 2010 car *42*

T
Taxes: avoiding import tax 29
  charity donations and **41**
  special concessions 29
Technology 38-39
  changes in *see* Innovation
Thunderbird car **39**, *39*
Tin Lizzie 17
Trademark **37**, *37*
Trade unions **23**
Traffic jams, first *17*
Training programs 23
Trotman, Alex *43*
Trucks 6

U
Union of Automotive Workers 23
United Way *40*,
US Leasing 33, *33*

V
Vans 6
  electric 43
Volkswagen "Beetle" *30*

W
Wages, daily rates 22
"Wall of Commitment" *43*
Whitney, Eli **18**
Whiz Kids 30, 31, 32
Wills, C. Harold 12
Winton, Alexander 11
World car 24

PRINTED IN BELGIUM BY

INTERNATIONAL BOOK PRODUCTION